Soccer
the Winning Way

GREYSTONE BOOKS

Douglas & McIntyre Publishing Group
Vancouver · Toronto · New York

Greystone Books
A division of Douglas & McIntyre Ltd.
2323 Quebec Street, Suite 201
Vancouver, British Columbia
Canada v5t 4s7
www.greystonebooks.com

Canadian Cataloguing in Publication Data

Mackin, Bob, 1970–
    Soccer the winning way

ISBN 1-55054-825-5

1. Soccer—Juvenile literature. I. Title
GV943.25.M32 2001   j796.334'2   C00-911380-0

Printed and bound in Hong Kong by
C&C Offset Printing Co. Ltd.
Printed on acid-free paper ∞

We gratefully acknowledge the financial support of the Canada Council for the Arts, the British Columbia Ministry of Tourism, Small Business and Culture, and the Government of Canada through the Book Publishing Industry Development Program (BPIDP) for our publishing activities.

Credits

Editing by Lucy Kenward
Cover and text design by Peter Cocking

Photography by Stefan Schulhof/
Schulhof Photography, except as indicated below:

Photos by Allsport:
Front cover photo by Jamie McDonald
Vincent Laforet: p. 5 · Claudio Villa: p. 11, p. 22
Ross Kinnaird: p. 12, p. 41 · Phil Cole: p. 15, p. 21
Nuno Correia: p. 16 · Ben Radford: p. 25
Shaun Botterill: p. 28, p. 31, p. 60
Andy Lyons: p. 32 · Stu Forster: p. 35, p. 42
Tom Hauck: p. 39 · Graham Chadwick: p. 47
David Durochik: p. 53 · Doug Pensinger: p. 54
David Leah: p. 59

Special thanks

The author would like to thank: Rob Sanders, Terri Wershler, Lucy Kenward, Peter Cocking, Stefan Schulhof, Derek Possee, Shel Brødsgaard, Bob Lenarduzzi, Anne Rose, Rick Anderson, Sue Anderson, Linda Knight and the North Shore Ice, Gareth Hughes, Brenda Reeves and the Mount Seymour Royals, Mark Parker and the Surrey United Selects, Saibo Talic, Jason Villeneuve, Clark deBoer, Quentin O'Mahony, Ajit Braich, Ach Bedouene, Peter Speck, Tim Renshaw, Neville Judd, Paul Dolan and Kathy McAusland of Umbro Canada, City of Burnaby Department of Parks and Recreation, the British Columbia Soccer Association, and Bob Mackin Sr. and Sherry Mackin. Thanks most of all to the many fine young players who made up our "winning way" team—and to their parents.

CONTENTS

THE WINNING WAY TEAM

Alex Kearney

Emily Knight

Hassan Mire

Brianna Calli

Robjinder Dhillon

Robbie Giezen

Jordan Miller

Trevor Wicken

Stephanie Weston

Pavan Bilin

Anthony Battistel

Erin Cheng

Kristen Anderson

Brian Sawatzky

Iain Gielty

Jesse Knight

Nicholas Mann

Devon Reeves

Sean Kearney

Graeme Tingey

James Clift

Anna LeGresley

Travis Anderson

Jitender Gill

Alison Youl

Kevin Hughes

Josh Barnes

Nick Boyd

Derek Luporini

Corey Bergen

Matthew deBoer

Cara Hutchison

Brandon Steuenberg

Brian Nekrash

Cameron Whitters

2

Derek Possee

Head coach, British Columbia Soccer Association

A former assistant coach of Canada's World Cup and Olympic teams, Derek Possee now trains British Columbia's top players. Before turning to coaching, Possee, though only five-foot-five, was a speedy striker and goal scorer with Tottenham Hotspur of England's first division. He also played for Milwall, Crystal Palace, and Leyton Orient before joining the North American Soccer League's Vancouver Whitecaps.

Bob Lenarduzzi

General manager, Vancouver Whitecaps

A coach of Canada's men's World Cup team from 1992 to 1997, Bob Lenarduzzi led the Vancouver Eighty-Sixers to four consecutive Canadian Soccer League titles. He anchored Canada's defense in the 1984 Olympics and 1986 World Cup. During his 11-year career with the original Vancouver Whitecaps, he played all 11 positions and the most games in North American Soccer League history. He is a member of Canada's Soccer Hall of Fame.

Shel Brødsgaard

Goalkeeping coach, Canadian under-16 and under-18 national women's youth teams

A former professional soccer player with Hvidovre F.C. in Denmark and five teams in the Canadian Soccer League, Shel Brødsgaard was a member of Canada's Olympic qualifying team in 1992. Brødsgaard now coaches provincial- and national-level goalkeepers, and teaches community-level coaches.

Mark Parker

Coach, British Columbia Soccer Association Provincial/National High Performance Centre and Academy of Soccer Education

A Union of European Football Associations (UEFA) B License coach, Mark Parker originally worked with the Northern Transvaal Football Association in South Africa. He now trains youth and senior players across British Columbia, and certifies local and provincial coaches.

Why is soccer so popular? Because it's fun, it moves quickly, and you can play almost anywhere, any time.

All you need is a space to play, two teams, and a ball. An open, flat, and rectangular grass field with goalposts at either end is ideal for a match. But you can also play soccer in gymnasiums, in playgrounds and alleys, and on the beach.

Practice often, play fair, treat your body well, and you'll be well on your way to having fun and playing like the pros. Just put on your jersey, lace up your boots, and get ready to play.

Kick off

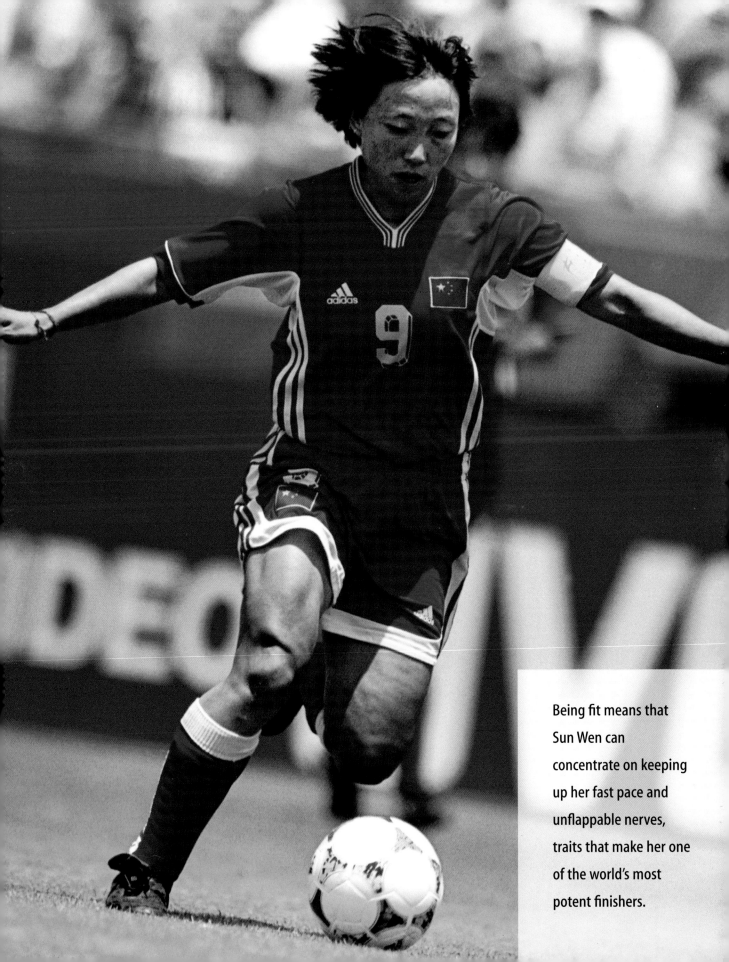

Being fit means that Sun Wen can concentrate on keeping up her fast pace and unflappable nerves, traits that make her one of the world's most potent finishers.

KIT AND EQUIPMENT

When your uniform fits properly, you can focus on the game, not on your clothes.

Goalkeeping gloves help to grip the ball. Snug the fasteners around your wrists.

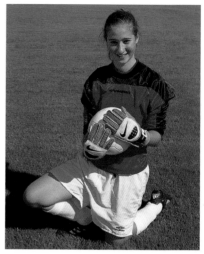

Squeeze the ball before the game starts. If it feels soft, let the referee know.

Choose your kit

If you're comfortably dressed, you'll probably play better. Depending on the time of year and the weather, your soccer jersey may be short or long sleeved. If you're a goalkeeper, your jersey will have elbow and shoulder padding for protection. Choose a jersey that's loose fitting but not too big and baggy. Tuck the jersey into your shorts.

Your soccer shorts may have an elastic waistband or a drawstring and should have a relaxed fit. If you're a goalkeeper, your shorts will have light thigh or hip padding to prevent injury. Tighten the drawstring, not just because it looks neat: you don't want your shorts to fall down when you run.

Remember to pull your socks up to your knees. They may not look so cool, but they'll keep your shinguards in place and prevent you from getting hurt. Some shin guards come in special "undersocks," which you can wear under your regular socks. Other models have built-in ankle guards for extra protection.

Fit your gloves

If you're a goalkeeper, you'll wear gloves with sticky grips to catch the ball. Your goalkeeping gloves should look bigger than your hands but make sure they don't slip off your wrists; the elastic band or the velcro fasteners should be firm. Make sure that you have a little bit of space at the end of your fingertips.

Shinguards are a must. Wear them over your shin bone but under your socks.

Pull up your socks and fasten your laces. Make sure the bow is on top of your foot.

Wrap your laces around the boot in the arch between the forefoot and the heel.

Choose your boots

Your soccer boots are made from lightweight leather with a molded plastic or rubber sole. The soles contain a series of cleats, or studs, which keep you from slipping on grass fields.

Check the fit. Make sure your feet are snug in the boots and that you have enough room to wiggle your toes. If you can fully bend your big toe inside the boot, it's too big. Walk quickly around the shoe store. If the boots don't feel right, try another model.

Feed the laces through the eyelets on the top of your boots, above the tongue, in a crisscross pattern like regular shoes. Lace firmly to the top eyelet for the most support and tie a double-bow on the outside of each boot. Or tie the laces around your boots, from the top of your foot to the sole and back around. Make sure the bow on top is secure.

Remove the grass or dirt from the soles of your boots after each practice or game. Wipe and polish your boots until they shine to soften the leather and make them last longer.

Choose the ball

A real soccer ball is a leather or plastic ball that is properly inflated with a pump and a special needle. Older kids and adults use a size five ball. Start with a size four, which is slightly smaller and lighter. Or if you're eight or nine years old, use a size three ball until you're comfortable with the game.

TIP

Well-kept, second-hand boots can sometimes be as good as a new pair. What's most important is how the boots feel on your feet.

FOOD AND FITNESS

Sit with your legs wide apart. Gently reach for your toes to stretch your hamstring muscles.

Stretch your groin muscles by folding one leg behind you. Extend the other leg and gently reach for your toes. Don't bounce. Switch legs and repeat.

Eat right

Your body is like an electric car that needs recharging every day. Eat a balanced diet and keep in mind these tips so that you have enough energy to play soccer:

- Eat a full breakfast every day to give you energy, but have a light breakfast before a morning game.
- Eat a full meal the night before a game or practice.
- Drink lots of water before, during, and after a game or practice so that you don't get dehydrated.
- Eat pasta and fruit after a game to refuel your empty tank.

Stay healthy

Stay active away from the soccer field. Hike, cycle, swim, play tennis, or try futsal, a form of soccer played indoors with fewer players.

To prevent injuries and make sure that you can play your best, set aside 20 minutes before a match or practice to lightly jog once around the field and stretch comfortably. Remember to warm up your whole body.

After the game, do some of the same exercises for five to 10 minutes to cool down—but use less force. Hold the stretches for 15 to 30 seconds to lengthen the muscles.

At the end of the day, make sure that you get enough rest.

Push hands with a teammate to stretch out your Achilles tendon. Use equal force.

Keep water and a snack on the touchlines. Refuel when you're not playing.

Shake hands with opponents and officials. Without them, you couldn't play a game.

Know your team

A winning team plays together and stays together. Get to know your teammates. Go for a meal after a game or go see a movie, and spend as much time as you can playing together.

Treat everyone with respect

Approach every practice and game with a positive attitude. Take a deep breath and think about how you can do your best to help your team. Respect the other team, its coaches and supporters, the referee and assistant referees.

The referee enforces the rules, which are known as the Laws of the Game. You may disagree with some calls, but the referee's decision is final. Don't get angry or upset—just keep playing to help your team succeed.

On the field (and off), treat everyone else like you want them to treat you. You wouldn't want to be tripped or pushed, especially while carrying the ball towards the other team's goal. So spend your energy kicking the ball, not your opponents.

When you score goals and win games it feels good, but losing should not be any less fun. Remember: it's only a game.

Win or lose, smile and shake hands with your opponents and thank the officials.

If you did your best and had a good time, you've got the right attitude. You're playing the winning way.

TIP

Two-thirds of your body weight is water. During a game, top players can lose 10 pounds/ 4.5 kg by sweating! Keep drinking water and you'll stay cool.

9

You're dressed for action. Your body and mind are sharp. You're prepared to practice or play. Time to kick off.

In a match, the game starts when the referee whistles to put the ball in to play. One player passes to a teammate over the halfway line at the center of the field. But that's just the beginning.

To keep the ball and take it forward to score a goal, you need to control it. You need to move the ball, pass it to your teammates, and receive it from them. If you can master the fancy footwork in this chapter, you'll soon be dribbling like Ronaldo, making tricky passes like David Beckham, and trapping the ball like Mia Hamm.

Ball control

Every striker needs confidence, and Christian Vieri has lots of it. His speed, agility, and power in the air mean that he can control the ball and create goals from nothing.

Ronaldo loves to play soccer, and he likes nothing more than scoring goals. It doesn't matter how you score, but you do have to be in the right place at the right time and know what to do.

Keep the ball between the insides of your feet to maintain control.

Chip the ball by stabbing your instep underneath it to lift it off the ground.

Keep the ball within reach, especially when you use the outsides of your feet.

Use your feet

Your feet carry you around the field at paces slow and fast. They also control the ball, pass and receive it, and shoot. So stay on your toes and be ready for anything.

- Use the curved inside parts of your feet to control the ball, dribble (or move), pass, and receive.
- Use the slightly sloped parts on top of each foot where your shoelaces are to chip (or lift) the ball or to shoot on goal.
- Use the outsides of your feet only when you want to go faster—controlling the ball this way can be tricky.

Keep the ball within reach

Don't push the ball ahead too far. You don't want to play catch-up and watch the ball roll away. Try to keep it 3 feet/1 m or slightly less ahead of you at all times.

Keep your head up

Keep your head up to anticipate changes in direction. Move your eyes from right to left and back again because defenders aren't likely to approach you head-on. Keep your ears open because you may be challenged from behind.

TIP

Slow down! Don't try to play the ball when you're moving too fast. The ball is much easier to control when your body is behind it and you have time to think about your next move.

BALL MOVEMENT DRILLS

Practice controlling the ball by weaving around cones. Keep it close by your toe.

Replace the cones with players. Feint with the ball.

Ask the players to move back and forth to provide more of a challenge.

Slalom drill

Set up 10 cones or pylons, spaced at 6-foot/2-m intervals in a zig-zag pattern. Dribble the ball around the obstacles with the insides of your feet first. For example, when going to the left of a pylon, use the inside of your right foot. When you feel confident, use the outside of your left foot. Then alternate between the inside and outside of each foot as you go around the obstacles. After rounding the last pylon, sprint with the ball straight back to the point where you started.

Feinting drill

Dribble the ball around the obstacle course again, this time move slower and replace the cones with three players at 15-foot/ 5-m intervals. Try feinting—faking a move to one direction and quickly going in another.

Look to your right and drop your shoulder in that direction. Suddenly move to your left while pushing the ball forward with the inside of your right foot. Speed up with the ball around the obstacles.

As you get better at controlling the ball, have your teammates move slowly from side to side. Expect that they'll try to block the ball as you carry it around them to an open space on the field.

Zinedine Zidane is firm in the tackle and powerful in the air. His dribbling ability can turn a game. But it's the pinpoint accuracy of his passes and crosses that sets him apart.

Roberto Carlos makes passes look easy. But he is best known for his free kicks. For those, he prefers to strike the ball with the outside of his left foot to make a booming, swerving shot.

Use the inside of your foot to pass along the ground. Plant your foot, look, pass.

Use the outside of your foot to change directions. Stay upright; don't lean back.

Use your instep to make powerful passes. Swing from your hip and snap your knee.

Keeping the ball for your team means passing the ball, moving up the field, and supporting your teammates. Share the ball: if you pass to your teammates, they'll pass the ball back to you.

Make the pass

In a game, quickly find the teammate closest to you but farthest from an opposing player.

To pass the ball, look squarely at where you want it to go. Position your non-kicking foot towards the target and center your weight over this foot. Transfer your weight to your passing foot to help propel the ball. Turn your hips towards your target and swing your foot as if it is the pendulum of a clock.

Strike the center of the ball with your foot and follow through with your whole leg moving away from your body like it's an arrow. Bull's-eye! After you've kicked the ball, your leg should point directly at the person the ball is going to. Keep your eye on the ball until you've kicked it.

Support the pass

If you don't have the ball, be ready to receive a pass by moving to support your ball-carrying teammate. You can be behind, ahead, or beside that player. The more players in support positions, the more options your team has to keep the ball moving.

TIP

Make shorter, more accurate passes. When you make a pass, every second counts. The faster the game, the more quickly you have to think before you play the ball.

RECEIVING

Use the sole of your foot to trap the ball.

Angle your thigh towards the ground at 45° and cushion the ball…

…then gently let the ball drop to the ground at your feet. Be ready to follow.

Be prepared

If you give, you will get. But receiving is not as simple as passing. Many passes aren't completed because the intended receiver isn't prepared. So, be ready to receive the ball at all times.

Know where your teammates and opponents are. Know who has the ball. Look for an open space away from your opponent.

Communicate with your teammates by waving your hands or even calling a name or a key word. Don't make yourself too obvious if you're in an open space or you'll soon be marked, and then your teammates won't pass you the ball.

When you receive the ball, position yourself behind it and use your body to stop it before you move, pass, or shoot.

Use your feet

As the ball moves towards the ground, raise one foot and then quickly, yet gently, lower it with the ball to the ground. Try to contact the ball with the inside or top of your foot. Keep your arms slightly raised for balance.

Use your thighs

When the ball is near waist level, pretend you are making a table for it to land on. Bend your knee to contact the ball, cushion it with the "meaty" part of your thigh, not the "bony" part of your knee, and straighten your leg. Let the ball drop to your feet.

Draw the ball into your chest by closing your shoulders. Let it fall to your feet.

Watch the ball as it falls. Jump up or step back so that it hits your eyebrows.

Let the ball drop to your feet and you'll be on your way!

Use your chest

To receive a high ball, use your chest like a shield. As the pass approaches, stretch your limp arms apart as if you are a bird with wings. Contact the ball with the middle of your chest, at about the same level as the bottom of your armpits. When the ball strikes, relax, arch your shoulders, and move them inward to drop the ball to the ground. Glance at your feet to line up the ball, then look up and forward again to avoid colliding with another player.

If you have time, simply stop in the path of the falling ball, bend your knees, and lean back to chest the ball. Let the ball roll to your feet.

Use your head

Receiving the ball with your head can be fun but challenging. To keep the ball from hitting you in the face, pretend you're catching it with the tops of your eyebrows. Keep your eyes on the ball.

As the ball approaches, lean back and bend your knees slightly. Put your head behind the ball in its downward path and keep your neck long. Think about throwing your eyes through the ball. Step back if the ball is too close and, as you hit the ball, relax your upper body to keep the ball under control.

If you hit the ball instead of letting it hit you, you'll have more control. Remember: don't let the ball strike the top of your head, because it will bounce away from you.

TIP

Heading doesn't have to hurt. Practice with a small, light ball. Keep your eyes wide open and your mouth sealed shut. Bend your neck, bite down with your teeth, and clench your jaw.

CHANGING DIRECTION

The more control you have...

...the faster you can change direction to fool an opponent.

Stop, change direction, and take a shot on goal. Or fool the goalkeeper.

Keep the other team guessing

You can't keep the ball for your team by traveling in a straight line, which is why stopping with the ball and changing directions is essential. Keep your opponents guessing about your every move. Change directions to get away from a marking player, then you can pass the ball to a teammate.

Change direction on the run

To change direction while moving, lean in one direction and drop your shoulder that way. Keep the ball away from your opponent by using your foot as a hook. Turn in the opposite direction and quickly take the ball that way.

Stop and change direction

You can also suddenly change direction (and the flow of the game) by speeding up, stopping quickly, and trapping the ball on the ground with the sole of one foot. Drag the ball back with the sole of your boot on top of the ball and twist your body to face where you want to go.

If you can change directions successfully, you'll leave your opponent in the dust while you move the play downfield.

If you're enthusiastic about soccer, you'll go far. Nwankwo Kanu grew up in Nigeria playing with bare feet and a rag ball. Today, he controls the ball with finesse.

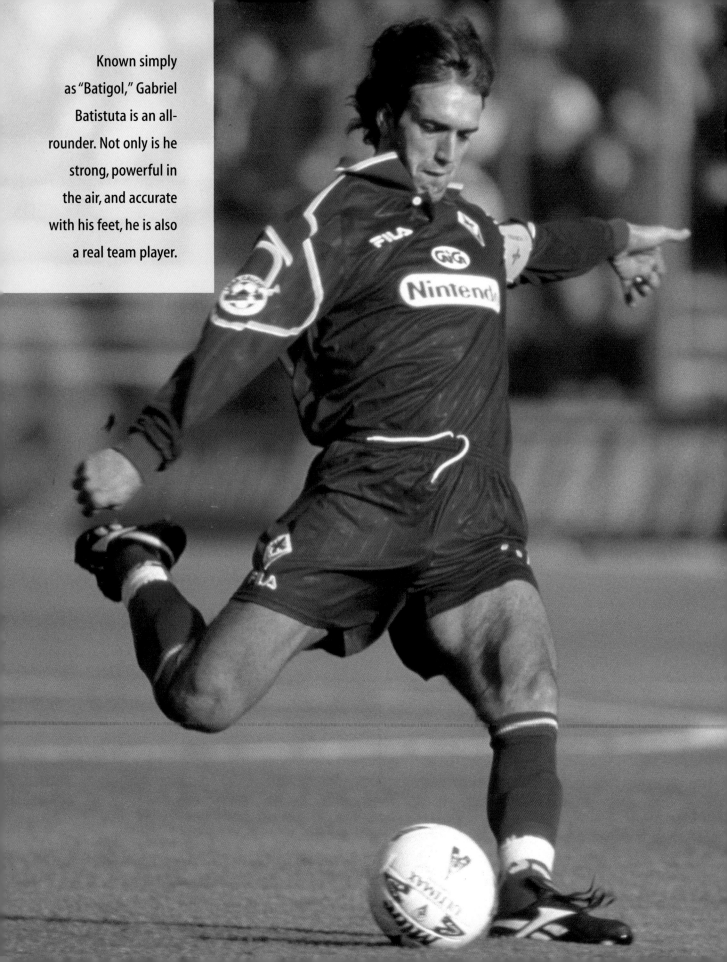

Known simply as "Batigol," Gabriel Batistuta is an all-rounder. Not only is he strong, powerful in the air, and accurate with his feet, he is also a real team player.

Practice changing direction with your teammates, using a two-on-one drill.

Watch the ball and your opponent. Can you pass to a teammate?

Practice speeding up or slowing down to meet the wall pass.

Keepaway drill

Try a two-on-one keepaway game. If you are the solitary player, your job is to intercept a pass or strip the ball away from your teammates. If you are one of the players with the ball, you can only touch it twice: once to receive and once to pass. When you lose the ball, you must try to get it back. Practice using a three-touch rule; use the second touch to change direction.

Wall-passing drill

Join two teammates on the field to test your passing and receiving skills with this drill, commonly called the "give-and-go" (or "one-two").

Stand at one end of the field with your teammates on your right side, separated by 6 feet/2 m each. As you move the ball downfield, the player in the middle should pretend to be an opponent and face you at an angle while trying to intercept the ball. Drop back slightly and pass the ball with the inside of your left foot to the player farthest from you.

The receiving player should stop quickly, receive the ball, and pass it forward at an angle. Run ahead to receive the ball.

In a game, use the wall pass to move the ball up the field. It is dangerous for defending teams. Practice this skill between the halfway line and the start of the penalty area.

You can dribble the ball, pass, and receive it with the best. But can you put all these moves together and prevent the other team from scoring?

Defense isn't a flashy job. You won't score as many goals as midfielders or forwards, but that doesn't matter because defensive skills are what really win a game. If every player on your team—even the forwards and midfielders—can take the ball away from an attacker, you're well on your way to winning the game.

If you like to get in the ball's way and surprise other players, then defense is the position for you. Follow the tips in this chapter and you'll learn all the tricks to being a great defender.

Playing defense

Height and strength help defender Marcel Desailly win balls. He uses his body to intimidate strikers, and his agility and accurate passing to move the ball around the field.

POSITIONING

Position yourself between the ball and your goal so your opponent can't score.

Approach the ball-carrying attacker from an angle…

…and be ready to help your teammate if he can't get the job done.

Survey the field

To be a good defender, you have to know where and when to defend the ball. In your mind, divide the field into thirds.

The attacking third begins midway between the halfway line and other team's penalty area and ends at their goal line. On either side of the halfway line is the midfield. Get ready to defend whenever the ball enters the part of the midfield closest to your goal.

Your defending third is where you will be tested the most. It runs from your goal line to an area just outside your penalty area.

Know your role

If you're a central defender, help the goalkeeper clear the ball from the penalty area by heading or kicking it away from the middle of the field and towards the wings (sides).

As a left or right defender, protect the wings and also cover for central defenders.

As a midfielder (or halfback), your position in the middle third of the field makes you a link between the defenders (or fullbacks) and the forwards. You have one of the busiest jobs on the field, because the ball is either coming or going. You're the "engine room" of the team.

If you're a forward, help to defend when needed, especially during corner kicks and free kicks.

Use your body to force the attacker to the touchline.

An attacker will try to shield the ball with her body...

...wait for an opening, then challenge. But be careful not to cause a foul.

Get ready

When you don't have the ball, concentrate on being in the right place at the right time. Watch the way the attacking players move with the ball. Go to the ball, get behind it, and try to stay between it and the goal. Once you're in a good position to defend, you've made the first step to getting control of the ball.

Move towards the ball

When you don't have the ball, be in your defensive stance—ready to go and get it. Bend your knees, center your weight above your feet, and keep your arms by your sides for balance. As you watch the ball, shift your weight in the direction of play—just like a tree blowing in the wind. Always be at an angle with the ball so that you can move in any direction.

If you're close to an attacker carrying the ball, force the player to move to an area you want to go to. It's a foul to touch the attacker with your hands, legs, or body, so use the shape of your body. Get in front of the attacker and block his or her space to move with the ball.

Try to force an attacker to the touchline. The less room your opponent has to move, the more easily you can steal the ball or force it out of bounds.

Remember to back up your goalkeeper whenever he or she moves towards the ball.

TIP

Don't get caught "ball watching." It is more important to mark a player than gather with your teammates around the ball.

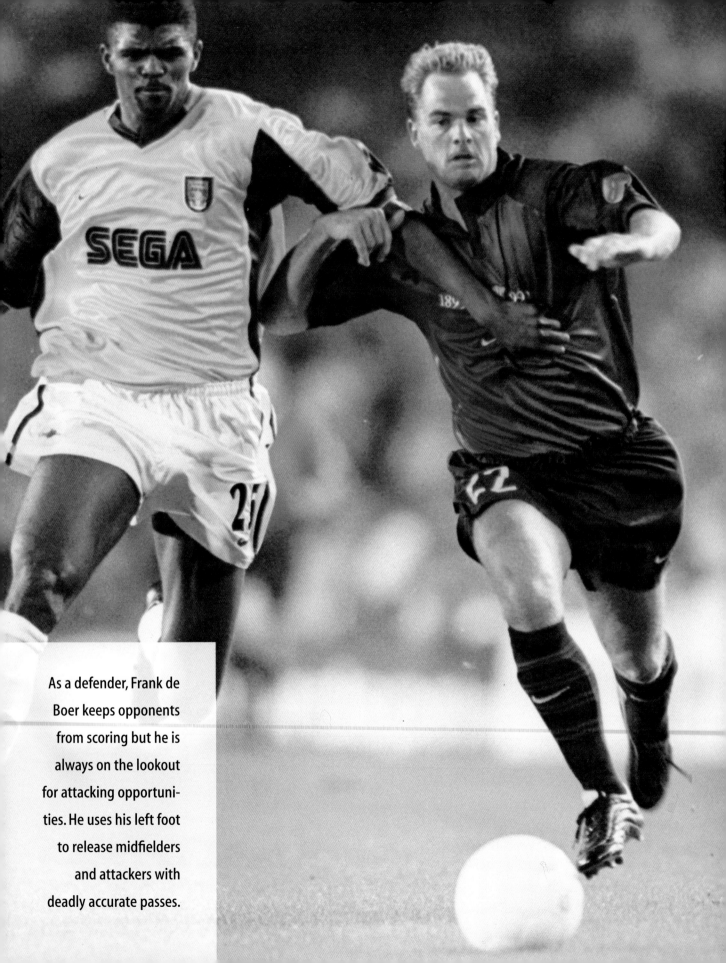

As a defender, Frank de Boer keeps opponents from scoring but he is always on the lookout for attacking opportunities. He uses his left foot to release midfielders and attackers with deadly accurate passes.

Stay close to your opponent when he has the ball. Watch his every move.

Prevent the ball from entering your zone by blocking an attacker or by challenging for the ball.

Stay in your zone, but force the attacker to go somewhere else.

Stay close

Marking means staying close to your opponent and standing so that your body blocks moves towards your goal. Go ahead and get in the way! Some teams use man (or player) marking; others prefer zonal marking.

Mark players

If you are marking a player, always stay with that person when you are defending. Stay within arm's length of your opponent but do not touch him or her with your legs, hands, arms, or upper body. Mark your player most closely when defending a corner kick, when he or she is waiting inside or just outside the penalty area to pounce on the ball.

Mark zones

If you are marking a zone, note where the attackers are positioned. Find a place in the penalty area away from your teammates and guard the space around where you stand. Challenge for the ball if it enters your area.

If you know how it works, marking a zone can be easier than marking a player. Instead of matching a player move for move, you watch the ball so that you can see better what is happening on the whole field. When you mark a zone, you are also much less likely to foul an attacker than when you mark a player.

DEFENSIVE STRATEGIES

Be ready in your defensive stance. Stay on your toes and watch the ball.

Use your body to force your attacker to his weak side.

Then pry the ball loose with a well-timed tackle.

Jockey your opponent

In soccer, jockeying has nothing to do with horses. It means staying with an attacker and moving into a position that will delay or destroy an attack.

To jockey, approach the attacker in your defensive stance but watch the ball, not the player's feet or body. Face the attacker at an angle and try to be within arm's reach. Stay between your opponent and the goal, and mark the attacker's strong side (the side he or she favors to move the ball). If you push the player to use the weak side, you can steal the ball or force an interception.

If the attacker tries to control the ball with his or her back to your goal, jockey to force the play to the weak side. The more pressure you apply, the less likely the attacker will be able to turn with the ball. If you don't get the ball first, the attacker will try to make a pass. If he or she turns, you can follow with a turn.

Tackle the ball

The first rule of tackling is always play the ball, not the player. To tackle, you take the ball away from your opponent with your feet. If you kick, push, or trip an attacker, you will be charged with a foul.

You can tackle from in front or beside a player but not from behind. Tackles from behind cause serious injuries and are against the Laws of the Game.

Oliver Bierhoff is strong in the air, scoring many goals with his head. His instinct allows him to be in the right place at the right time, but he says he succeeds because he believes in himself.

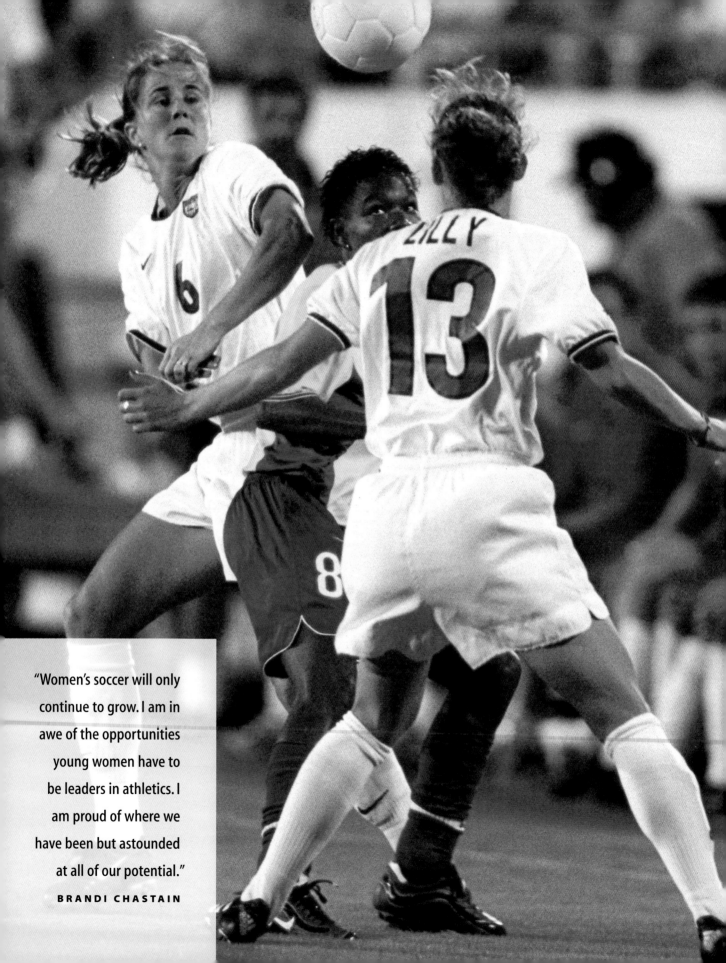

"Women's soccer will only continue to grow. I am in awe of the opportunities young women have to be leaders in athletics. I am proud of where we have been but astounded at all of our potential."

BRANDI CHASTAIN

Use a sliding tackle only as a last resort when the ball is out of reach. Approach from the side and bend your knee…

…then slide your tackling leg along the ground past the ball. Curl your foot around the ball to take it away.

Make a tackle

When an opponent is dribbling down the field or has just received the ball but hasn't controlled it, position yourself for a tackle. Move towards the attacker, plant one foot beside the ball, and kick your other leg towards the ball. Lean in to the tackle but don't push with your upper body. Use your arms for balance.

Trap your opponent offside

When you are defending the ball in your half of the field, you or one of your teammates should stay close to your goalkeeper. If the other team moves towards the goal, you can help your goalkeeper to trap the ball or kick it away.

When the ball comes into your half, watch the lead attacker and supporting players closely. Are they moving too quickly in your defensive third? If so, look to see which player might run for a pass. Is that player running past you or the teammate closest to your goalkeeper? If so, let him or her go. If the ball carrier tries a pass to that open player, then an assistant referee will rule the play offside. The game will stop, and your team will get an indirect free kick.

The offside trap doesn't always work so use it only after lots of practice. If the attacker is paying attention, he or she will either shoot directly or continue dribbling the ball until it's safe to pass.

TIP

Always stay on your feet as long as possible, no matter how you tackle the ball. Time a sliding tackle so that you get up as soon as you have the ball.

CLEARING THE BALL

Clear the ball in-bounds with a chip shot to send it far. Aim down the side of the field, away from the other team.

If an attacker is marking you closely, hit the ball out of bounds as far as possible from your goal.

TIP

If you can clear the ball out of bounds, send it over the touchline rather than the goal line. A throw-in is easier to defend against than a corner kick.

What is clearing the ball? It's when you quickly move the ball away from your third of the field just after taking it away from the other team.

Clear in bounds

If you can clear the ball and keep it in play, kick it high, long, and wide: high in the air, a long distance, and wide away from the other team. Avoid clearing the ball through the center of the field.

You can also clear a high ball using your head, but be careful that you don't butt heads with an opponent. You don't want to knock yourself out! Look at the ball and face whatever direction you want to go. With your arms by your sides for balance, jump towards the ball, and strike it with your forehead, just above your eyebrows. Keep your eyes open and your mouth closed.

The higher the ball, the farther you can make it go from your opponent. Just remember that a longer kick is harder to place accurately than a shorter one.

Clear out of bounds

If you're not ready or able to control the ball, and none of your teammates are nearby, clear it out of bounds over the touchline. The attacking team will get the ball but, during the brief pause, your team can regroup and move into a better defensive position.

As a playmaker, Hidetoshi Nakata tries to imagine the game the way spectators see it—from above. He says this aerial view helps him find open players or give attackers balls to run onto.

SET PLAYS

On a free kick, a human wall blocks the part of the goal closest to the kicker; the goalkeeper covers the far side.

When the shot comes, know what to do and listen to your goalkeeper. The closest defender should move to win the ball.

TIP

Always listen to your goalkeeper during set plays. Place your body between the ball and the goal during a free kick or a corner kick to block any shots that come your way.

Defend against a free kick

A free kick restarts the game when a team has been fouled. If the other team was fouled, be ready for a free kick from one of your opponents.

Your goalkeeper may arrange a human wall to block a large, empty portion of your goal. The closer the ball and the kicker are to the center of the goal, the more of you there will be in the wall.

Line up shoulder-to-shoulder with your teammates 10 yards/ 9.15 m away from the ball. Cast your head down but keep your eyes on the ball and the shooter. With your hands, cover your chest if you're a girl or your groin if you're a boy, so that you don't get hurt. Remain still until after the ball is kicked.

Stay together in the wall as long as possible after the free kick to prevent a goal. Then if you are the player closest to where the ball was struck, go to the ball and gain control. If you are farther away from the ball, mark your opponent.

Defend against a corner kick

A corner kick restarts the game when a defender touches the ball and it goes over his or her own goal line, either beside the goalposts or over the crossbar. If your team pushed the ball out of bounds, one of your opponents will take a kick from a small area where the touchline meets the goal line.

On a corner kick, mark opponents in the penalty area. Stay close to the goalposts to help the goalkeeper. Move immediately to defend the ball when it has been hit.

Mark the attacker closest to the throw-in. You'll make it harder to restart play.

Look out for the two swingers! An *inswinger* is a curved kick towards the goalposts. Your goalkeeper may have to work fast to make a save. An *outswinger* is a curved kick towards the edge of the penalty area. Be on your toes to clear the ball and prevent a shot on goal.

An attacker will sometimes make a short, quick kick to a teammate who can dribble the ball into a better position. If more than one attacker lines up at the corner, expect this play.

Two defenders should stand in front of either goalpost. Be ready to cover the space ahead of and behind the goalkeeper. Your other teammates should mark players or zones, at least 10 yards/ 9.15 m away from the ball until it has been struck.

Defend against a throw-in

A throw-in restarts the game when the ball goes over one of the touchlines. If your team puts the ball out of bounds, an opponent will throw the ball back into play.

Look to see which player is best able to receive the throw. That player is usually the one closest to the thrower but farthest from an opponent. Distract the thrower by moving side to side. Watch the thrower's body closely and try to guess which way the ball will go. The rest of your teammates should mark players. Don't forget to mark the thrower once he or she has released the ball.

TIP

Never use your hands or lower arms (only your goalkeeper can handle the ball) and never foul an attacker in the penalty area. If you do, the other team will earn a penalty kick—a one-on-one shootout against your goalkeeper.

You can run down the field, invade the other team's half, and fake the ball around other players. Now what? To win the game you need to attack and score goals.

Putting the ball between the goalposts is what soccer is all about. And it's a lot of fun. But just being in the right place doesn't mean that you'll score. You need to know where to stand, how to shoot, and what to think about.

It takes practice and lots of help from your teammates to score. So warm up your legs, fire up your reflexes, and get ready to shoot.

On the attack

Mia Hamm's speed and athleticism are constant dangers for any opponent. She is rarely out of the action, always contributing in attack while also chasing back to help out in defense.

POSITIONING

As he dribbles up the field towards two attackers, support your teammate by moving into an open space…

…so that you can receive a pass and move towards the goal for a chance to score.

TIP

Attack from the wings. Use one of your defenders to bring the ball up the side of the field. If you stand near the penalty area waiting to receive a pass, you'll be ready to strike.

Survey the field

To be a good attacker, you have to know where and when to shoot the ball. Attacking takes place in the other team's half of the field, especially around the penalty area. The more your team has the ball, the greater your chance to score.

As an attacker, always pass and move in a direction that feels comfortable. If you have to, backtrack into the middle third of the field with the ball before trying to get past the other team's defenders.

Look for ways to distract the defenders, move into open spaces, and be ready to receive a pass. If you're not carrying the ball, provide support in front, behind, and to the sides of the player who has the ball.

Know your role

The lead attacker is the player with the ball. It is often a forward, but it can be a midfielder or even a defender. It might even be you. You can attack alone, but always be aware of other players and the goal. It will be easier to keep the ball moving forward if a teammate follows to support you.

If a defender challenges you, your teammate should be close by, ready to receive a pass or distract the defender and continue the attack.

Forward Davor Suker is blessed with a sweet left foot and a powerful shot. But it's his excellent ball control and his trickery that can leave opponents wondering how to stop him.

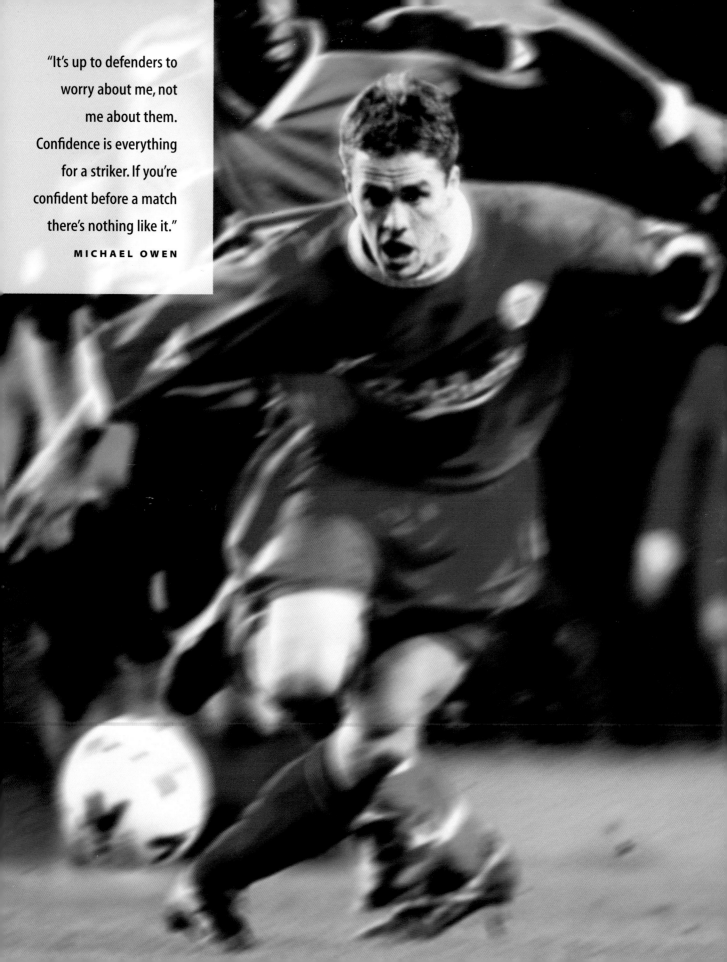

"It's up to defenders to worry about me, not me about them. Confidence is everything for a striker. If you're confident before a match there's nothing like it."

MICHAEL OWEN

Fool your marker by running away from your teammate and the ball. Then cut back across the field to receive a pass.

Move towards the center of the goal to wait for a cross; be careful to stay onside.

Position yourself for a pass

When you don't have the ball, trick the other team. Run away from the play! But don't run just anywhere. Run diagonally across the field into an open space ahead of the ball. Then you can receive a pass.

If you arrive too early or too late, you'll miss the ball and you could be offside. To time your run properly, go forward at an angle as the ball is played. Meet the ball just as it arrives behind the other team's defenders.

Move the ball up the field

If you are a forward or a midfielder, use the wall pass to move the ball up the field. Pass it back and forth around the other team's defender. At midfield, you can use a through pass. Send the ball forward in a straight line through a set of defenders. Aim for a teammate who is near the goal to receive the pass.

Support your teammates

If your lead attacker is running up the side of the field and gets trapped behind a wall of defenders, he or she may cross the ball into the middle of the penalty area. Move towards the near goalpost. Remain onside and wait for the cross. If the ball comes your way, you could be one touch away from scoring a goal!

TIP

Draw your marker away from the play by pretending that you're about to receive a pass. When you run off the ball, you leave your marker behind and help your teammates by being ready to receive a pass.

SHOOTING

Keep your eye on the ball and go to it at an angle.

Plant one foot beside the ball and swing the other leg back. Lean into the kick.

Strike the ball in the center and follow through with your whole body.

TIP

Watch for rebounds. After a shot, the ball could bounce off the goalkeeper, a defender, the goalpost, or the crossbar. Go to the ball and try to score. The quicker you are, the more you'll catch the defending team by surprise.

Master the basics

Stop, swing, strike: these are the three S's of shooting. Approach the ball at an angle, with the inside of your kicking foot facing the ball. Aim your other foot at the target, stop, and plant it beside the ball.

Swing your kicking leg back, bend it at the knee, then move your shoulders forward at the same time as your kicking knee. Keep your toes pointed down and your eyes on the ball.

Strike the top half of the ball with the inside of your foot. Kick with the fleshy part that curves outward, between your big toe and your instep.

Kick the ball low and hard by keeping your shoulder and kicking knee over the ball. Don't look up until you've hit the ball, then follow the shot towards the goal.

Attack with a volley

Volley the ball when you're moving and you want to kick it hard and long at the goal while it's still in the air. Don't put the ball over the net.

Watch the ball as it moves towards you in an arc. Get behind it, plant one foot, and swing your other foot towards the ball. Keep your toes pointed down and strike the center of the ball with the top of your foot, just where your laces are. Shift your weight forward suddenly as you kick. Keep the ball traveling low.

Watch the ball as it arcs towards you so that you can guide it onto your laces...

...Keep your toes down and strike the ball at its center to volley. Follow through.

For a half volley, kick the ball the second it bounces off the ground.

Attack with a half volley

Use a half volley when the ball is bouncing off the ground and you want to shoot at the goal.

A half volley is a lot like a karate kick. Get behind the ball and plant one foot. Lift your other leg and turn your knee sideways to the ground. Point your toes towards the goal and swing your foot into the kick. Strike the center of the ball along your shoelaces, keeping your kicking foot parallel to the ground. As you hit the ball, twist your upper body away from the shot. Use your arms to help keep your balance. When you follow through, your toes will be pointing away from the route that the ball takes.

Attack with a banana kick

You can strike a ball to make it curve like a banana. Use this kick around a defensive wall on a free kick or when you're rushing towards the goal.

Get behind the ball and center your weight on your non-kicking side. Lean back and swing your leg forward with your toes pointing up. Strike the ball with the fleshy part of your foot between your big toe and your instep. Hit the ball low to lift it high, with lots of spin and curve. If you do it right, the direction of the ball and your follow through will be completely different.

TIP

Test your shooting skills with a game of two-on-two in the penalty area. While the goal-keeper guards the net, you and your fellow attacker can only touch the ball twice each. Three touches and the defending pair becomes the attacking pair. The first pair to score 10 goals wins.

FINISHING PLAYS

A cross to an unmarked teammate can get the ball past a defender and finish a play.

Know where the goalkeeper is and shoot where he isn't. Take advantage of open space and score a goal!

Go for it

How you finish a play is often more important than how it started. If you have the ball and are in a position to score, go for it.

To successfully finish a play, look down at the ball, go to it at an angle, and use your arms for balance. Make sure that you're in a good position to score and keep your eye on the ball.

Control the ball

If the ball is bouncing along the ground or flying through the air, use your body, legs, or head to make the first touch for control. Or, if you can, control the ball and shoot it all with one touch.

Make the play

Glance at the goal. Where's the goalkeeper? Where are the defenders? The more space there is between you and the goalkeeper, the more of the field you have to work with. Get behind the ball and keep your eye on it. If the goalkeeper moves towards you, think fast. Pass to a teammate. Or dribble the ball away and hope to catch the goalkeeper off balance.

Remember: If you have control, look around, take aim, and then shoot. Always shoot for an open space. Finish with your toes pointing towards the crossbar.

"Believe that you can do something different from other players. Then find some space on the field and, if the ball comes to you, try to do something different."

RIVALDO

SET PLAYS

Jockey for space on a corner kick. Have at least one player by the near goalpost and another in the center of the goal area to tip the ball in. Keep the defenders guessing.

With the inside of your foot, kick the side of the ball for an inswinger.

When the ball goes out of bounds or the referee stops play, the ball will change hands. If you're taking a set play, be calm and concentrate. If you're too rushed, you'll make the wrong decision and the other team will get the ball.

Make a corner kick

When an opponent puts the ball out of bounds over the goal line, your team will be awarded a corner kick.

From the nearest spot where the touchline meets the goal line, place the ball inside the corner circle and leave the flag in place. Your teammates should be ready to receive a pass or to help tip the ball into the goal.

Corner kick checklist

- Use an inswinger (a curved kick towards the goal) to put the ball close to the goalmouth where your teammates can knock it in with their heads.
- Use an outswinger (a curved kick away from the goal) to reach the middle or shallow part of the penalty area, where your teammates can meet the ball with a volley, half volley, or header.
- Use a short pass to a teammate or use a direct straight-line drive from the corner into the penalty area to save time.

Do the same for an outswinger but aim away from the goalposts. Follow through.

On a penalty kick, shoot to the corners of the goal and at ground level . . .

. . . or aim above the goalkeeper's waist. Stay calm and focus.

Make a penalty kick

When the other team is defending and commits a serious physical foul or handball in its own penalty area, or when you're tied with another team in a tournament or playoff match, your team will get a penalty kick.

If you're taking the kick, it's just you against the goalkeeper. Until you kick the ball, the goalkeeper can move sideways but not forward from the goal line. And the other players have to stay behind you outside the penalty area.

Place the ball 12 yards/11 m away from the goal line on a white spot in the middle of the penalty area. Stay calm and focus on your shot, not on what the goalkeeper is doing. Decide where you want your shot to go and don't change your mind. Take three or four steps behind the ball at an angle. Strike the ball at its center with your stronger kicking foot. Kick hard and low.

Once you've kicked the ball, the other players will rush into the penalty area to pounce on a rebound. Be ready for your own second-chance kick if the ball bounces off the goalkeeper. If it hits the goalposts or the crossbar, wait until another player touches the ball before you go after it.

SET PLAYS

On a direct kick, aim over or around the wall. Follow through.

On an indirect kick, wait for a short pass from a teammate...

...then take your shot. Be quick or a defender will mark you.

Make a free kick

Wherever the referee spots a violation of the Laws of the Game by the other team, your team will get a free kick.

Expect a *direct* free kick when a player commits a serious physical foul or a handball. You can score a goal directly from a free kick. Anticipate an *indirect* free kick when a player commits a less serious foul. You can score a goal only after the kicker and at least one other player have touched the ball.

To make a free kick, look around. How are the defenders lined up in the defensive wall? Where is the goalkeeper? Where are your teammates? If you see a hole in the wall or a teammate without a marker, aim your shot there.

Make a drop ball

When a play was stopped, no foul has been called, and no one is sure who's in control of the ball, one player from each team will face off on a drop ball.

If you take the drop ball for your team, look around before the ball drops. Do you want to pass to an open teammate? Could you curl your foot around the ball and turn with it in the opposite direction? Decide what to do and don't change your mind.

If you are taking a drop ball because a player from the other team was injured, let your opponent win the drop ball.

Play starts again when the ball touches the ground.

On a throw-in, bring the ball straight over your head with both hands…

…and let the ball go when it's above your head. Keep your feet on the ground.

Throw to your closest open teammate, but make sure she's ready for the pass.

Throw the ball in

When the other team puts the ball out of bounds over the touch-line, your team restarts play with a throw-in. This is the only time you can play the ball with your hands (unless you're a goalkeeper).

Line up where the ball left play and face the field. Grip the ball with both hands, spreading out all 10 fingers to hold it steady. Swing the ball over and behind your head. Arch your back comfortably and step back with one foot or both. Keep your feet planted on the ground and your toes behind the touchline.

Look for an unmarked teammate who has space to move. When you're ready to throw the ball, stride towards the line, keeping your eyes fixed on your target. Throw your upper body ahead from its arching position, move both arms forward, and release the ball. Throw to your teammate's feet or chest so that he or she has the best chance to control the ball. Wait until another player hits the ball before you touch it again.

Receive a throw-in

When your teammate takes a throw-in, quickly find an open space on the field close to where the ball is being thrown in. If you're fast, you could receive the ball and move up the field before the other team knows what's happened. If you're being marked, move around to get away from your defender. Keep your eyes open to receive the ball or support your teammates.

TIP

Help the player receiving the ball on a throw-in decide what to do next. If he or she is being marked, shout "man on." Say "turn" if your teammate should turn to meet the ball.

You've been watching the pros jump, dive, and roll for the ball. They make keeping the ball out of the goal look easy. Can you make the saves? Are you up for the challenge?

It takes a special player to be a good goalkeeper. Not only do you need to be strong and fast on your feet like the rest of your teammates, you've got to have fancy fingers too. And that's not all. Goalkeepers are leaders. Besides blocking shots on goal, you have to make snap decisions and direct plays.

If your defenders are doing their job, you won't have much work. If they're having a bad game and you can stop the shots when it really counts, then you can save the day.

Goal keeping

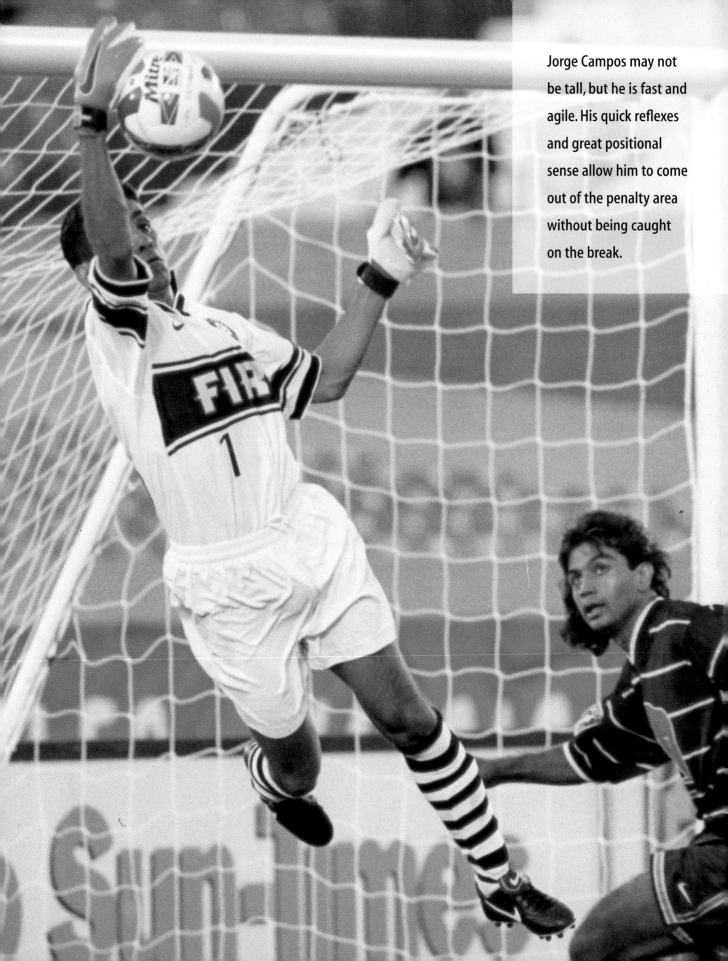

Jorge Campos may not be tall, but he is fast and agile. His quick reflexes and great positional sense allow him to come out of the penalty area without being caught on the break.

"I'm probably not the most athletic player, but I have a good work ethic. If my coach wants me to work on something, I'll work on it until I can perfect it."

NICCI WRIGHT

Start with a figure-eight drill to warm up your hands and fingers.

Practice reaching for the ball. Fall from your knees onto your hips.

Grip the ball with both hands, draw it into your chest, and curl your body around it.

After you've stretched with your teammates and relaxed your muscles, jog around the penalty area, pausing to skip or shuffle. Alternate between long strides and short steps. Go forward for a while, then move sideways.

Pretend to receive the ball. Reach both hands high above your head while moving. Then reach down to the ground with both hands.

Try your hands at these other fun drills:

Figure-eight drill

Stand still, spread your legs, and bend forward. Hold the ball with one hand and pass it around one leg and into your other hand just below your knees. Continue in a figure-eight pattern. Don't drop the ball!

Diving drill

Kneel 9 feet/3 m away from a teammate. Roll the ball back and forth, away from each other's body. Keep it slightly out of reach. Collapse down on the outside of your hip to where the ball is. Reach out with your hands to grip the ball: place one hand on top of the ball, place your other hand right behind the ball, and use the ground as your "third hand." Bring the ball into your chest as you fall to your side and land on the outside of your shoulder. Slide your top leg over the ball to protect yourself.

TIP

Practice jumping like a frog and pretend the ball is like a fly. Your hands and body are like a frog's tongue and mouth. Catch the ball! The penalty area is your pond and the goal is your lily pad. Don't let any balls land there!

POSITIONING

In your ready position: weight over your toes, knees and elbows slightly bent.

Keep your body between the ball and the goal. Catch the ball with your hands.

Always look and listen to the play, wherever it is. Be ready to move quickly.

TIP

Always look prepared. When you're in the proper stance— when it's just as easy to jump as it is to collapse to the ground—attackers will think twice about shooting.

Survey the field

Just as your teammates pretend the field has three parts, divide the third that contains your penalty area into three sections. When the ball is in the attacking third, stand at the top or ahead of the penalty area. When the ball enters the midfield, be ahead of the goal but within the penalty area. And when the ball comes into your defending third, stay between the goal and the goal line.

Any ball that goes into the penalty area should be yours, unless you let a teammate have it. Stand off the goal line in the middle of the goal only during a corner kick. At other times, keep your eye on the ball and be ready to get into position for a play.

Get ready

Stand with your legs shoulder-width apart. Center your knees over your feet, and balance your weight on the balls of your feet, not on your heels. Gently lean forward with your arms extended and your elbows slightly bent at waist level. Face your palms out towards the shooter and spread your fingers in a ready position. Focus on the game.

Get in position

No matter how good you are at handling the ball, being in the right place is the only way to make a save. Always be behind the ball. Opponents should see you in the ready position with your

Move forward to look bigger to the shooter. Stay inside the penalty area.

Cut down the shooter's angle by blocking the goal with your body.

When the time is right, jump on the ball. Keep it in front of you.

palms out, and your back should always face the goal. Otherwise, you might turn around for a big surprise.

To be in the correct position, start in the center of the goal. Since your body blocks only a part of the goal, your best bet is to cover whatever area of the goal you can. Then move forward carefully but confidently.

Move towards the ball

Find the ball and draw an imaginary line from it through the middle of your legs to the middle of the goal. Face the ball and stand a safe distance off the goal line. You may want to move forward 13 to 20 feet/4 to 6 m or just take a few steps ahead. Judge how fast the ball and your attacker are moving, and run forward to narrow the angle.

Challenge your attacker

Challenge an opponent in a one-on-one situation to keep the attacker from coming to you. When you narrow the angle or close the distance between you and the attacker, you will appear bigger and the goal smaller. The attacker will have less time and space to make a shot. If you're too far out of the goal, a simple chip shot over your head could score a goal.

A good goalkeeper will save a shot. A great goalkeeper can prevent a shot from being made.

TIP

Focus on the game in front of you. As you watch the ball and the players, think about what plays could come next. Who might try a shot on goal? How could you block it? If you're mentally prepared, you'll be ready to make the save.

MAKING THE SAVE

Catch a low ball ahead of your grounded knee. Bring the ball into your chest.

Form the letter W with your hands to meet the ball at its highest point.

When diving, catch the ball with one hand above and one below.

TIP

React to a shot when it has been made. Don't guess where the shooter is sending the ball *before* the kick. This is especially true on a penalty kick. That's when your reaction time will be put to the test.

Catch a low ball

Get behind a low ball as it rolls or bounces to waist level. Point your fingers towards the ground with your thumbs to the sides. Together your hands should be shaped like a shovel, ready to dig any ball that comes your way. You should see the palms of your hands as you reach out your arms to meet the rolling ball. Go down on one knee and scoop up the ball. Cradle the ball in your hands, fold your shoulders in, and hug it to your chest.

Jump for a high ball

You may need to jump to meet a ball at chest or shoulder level. Get behind the ball's path and reach up with your arms. Hold your hands together, palms out, and fingers pointed up and spread apart so that your index fingers and thumbs make the letter W. Grab the ball in mid-air. Once the ball is in your hands, draw it into your chest. Always try to catch the ball at its highest point and finish a save with the ball tucked safely into your chest.

Dive for a ball

If the ball is away from your body, dive or jump at it with your arms outstretched. Always try to catch the ball with two hands. Punch or push the ball away from the goal to the sides. Get back on your feet as fast as you can.

Craig Forrest is agile between the posts and knows exactly where to position himself off the goal line. With skills like these, he is happy to take some chances to help his team win.

"I love the freedom that the goalkeeper position allows you. But I also love the responsibility that goes with the job. I feel the same pressure as the others, but I handle it differently."

FABIEN BARTHEZ

Roll the ball along the ground like you are bowling…

…or hurl it over your shoulder for more force.

Drop the ball, kick it on the way up just after it bounces…

…and follow through with your leg and your whole body.

As soon as you make a save, get back on your feet and help build your team's attack on the goalkeeper at the opposite end. Use throws to cover shorter distances more accurately and use kicks for longer distances.

Throw the ball

An overhand hurl will go farther than an underhand bowl. Use whichever throw will reach your closest open teammate. Look for a player along the sides of the field because an attacker can intercept a throw across the middle, giving the other team a chance to score.

Kick the ball

As a goalkeeper, you should have the same footwork skills as other players—if not better! Use a punt or drop kick to send the ball long distances and to clear it quickly. You may catch the defending team off guard, especially if your teammates are moving up the field.

Hold the ball with both hands. Take two or three steps. Lean forward, lower the ball, and kick it out of your hands. Strike it with the top of your foot. After you have used all your force and followed through, your body should feel like it is falling back.

TIP

If a goalkeeper handles the ball for more than six seconds, or handles a pass or a throw-in from a teammate, the other team will get an indirect free kick where the foul took place.

COMMUNICATION

Communicate with your team. Shout instructions, warnings, and encouragement. Signal plays or point out where a defender should stand, especially during set plays.

Don't forget to thank your opponents for a game well played.

As a goalkeeper, you are an important leader because you are the only player with a full view of the field. As you see play developing, tell your teammates what you see and where they should be. Warn and encourage your teammates by name so that they will know who you are talking to.

Communication checklist

- Shout "man on" if you see a player being marked or challenged.
- If a teammate is blocking your view during an opponent's attack, shout "screen."
- Shout "keeper" to let everyone know that you will be challenging to get the ball.
- If you're not going after the ball, shout "away" so that one of your teammates can clear the ball.

Set a good example

Your teammates will look for your direction and encouragement. Think positively and maintain a good attitude, and the other players will too. If you allow a goal, don't be angry. The more agitated you are, the less focused you'll be on the game. And you need to concentrate so that the other team doesn't score again. Learn from your mistakes so that goals and bad games are rare.

When you do make a save, celebrate with your teammates. After all, you're a winning team and you've all played your best.